WRITTEN ENGLISH FOR BUSINESS

First level

Preparing for the LCCI Examinations

WRITTEN ENGLISH FOR BUSINESS

First level

Alan Stanton

OXFORD UNIVERSITY PRESS

Oxford University Press
Great Clarendon Street, Oxford OX2 6DP

Oxford New York
Athens Auckland Bangkok Bogota Bombay
Buenos Aires Calcutta Cape Town Dar es Salaam
Delhi Florence Hong Kong Istanbul Karachi
Kuala Lumpur Madras Madrid Melbourne
Mexico City Nairobi Paris Singapore
Taipei Tokyo Toronto

and associated companies in
Berlin Ibadan

OXFORD and OXFORD ENGLISH are trade marks of
Oxford University Press

ISBN 0 19 451232 0

Typeset by Oxford University Press
Printed in Hong Kong

CONTENTS

INTRODUCTION

I HOW TO USE THIS BOOK

This book may be used in class, or for individual study. It shows you a past English for Business First Level paper, and then takes the four types of question in the paper in turn. This is how you can use the different sections for each of the four questions:

- Read the Sample Question
- Read the 'Approach' section
- Write your answer to the Sample Question
- Compare your answer with the Sample Answers and Comments
- Read the Summary of Common Errors
- Answer the Further Practice question, covering the answers until you have completed it.

For further practice, you might then answer the questions at the end of the book, and finally attempt the complete past paper at the end of this Introduction. Other past papers can be obtained from the London Chamber of Commerce Examinations Board, to enable you to practise not only individual questions but also the effective use of time under examination conditions.

2 WHAT THE EXAMINER IS LOOKING FOR

What is the examiner looking for when marking an English for Business First Level paper?

Throughout the paper, there is a greater emphasis on comprehension rather than production of English. Apart from Question 1, candidates do not have to write a great deal: what is needed is careful reading of instructions and accurate execution of the tasks set. There follows an analysis of each question-type.

QUESTION I

This is a memo or letter within or between business organizations. It is important to know the layout of memos and letters well, and not to confuse the two. This question is the only one which requires continuous prose. The examiner awards marks for appropriate style in addition to accurate grammar and punctuation. Most important, however, is to achieve the objective set: if the task was to inform people of a meeting, you will not get good marks for omitting vital information such as time, place, and date, even if you have made few errors in your use of language.

QUESTION 2

The examiner is looking for brief, accurate answers to questions on the passage. Comprehension is more important than production of accurate English here. In particular, you should be able to connect information which occurs in different parts of the passage.

QUESTION 3

The idea is to 'look and think', using the graphic, numerical or quantitative display and interpreting from it in order to give brief answers to the question. In many cases, your answer will be a number or percentage; you will certainly not need full sentences.

QUESTION 4

This is a 'look and write' task. The examiner is looking for the ability to understand and complete a chart, form, or diagram or to re-order given information and data.

3 SAMPLE PAPER

FIRST LEVEL

THE LONDON CHAMBER OF COMMERCE AND INDUSTRY

SERIES 3 EXAMINATION

ENGLISH FOR BUSINESS

(CODE No: 1041)

INSTRUCTIONS TO CANDIDATES

(a) *Answer all four questions.*

(b) *Credit will be given for correct spelling, punctuation and grammar, as well as appropriate style and relevant content.*

(c) *Adequate and appropriate communication is required rather than a particular number of words.*

(d) *When you finish, check your work carefully.*

QUESTION 1

Situation: The monthly photocopying bill for your company has recently increased enormously. As Office Manager, you must do something about this, but at the moment it is impossible to check how many photocopies each employee is making each month.

You have decided to fit a 'Copygard' to the photocopier. This is a small computer which keeps a record of how many photocopies each employee makes. Each employee will have a six-figure personal access number and this must be typed into the 'Copygard' in order to switch the photocopier on. The photocopier will not work if the access number is not typed into the 'Copygard' and so anyone without a number will not be able to use it.

Task: Write a **memo** to all employees. Include the following information in your memo:

(a) An explanation of the problem with the photocopier.

(b) Your views on the cause of this problem.

(c) What you are doing to overcome this problem.

(d) A brief explanation of how the system will come into operation.

(e) Details of when the new system will come into operation.

(f) A tear-off slip at the bottom of the memo for employees to return to you. This must show the employee's name, job and the six-figure access number they have chosen.

Set the memo out appropriately, using today's date. You should make up other useful information (e.g. photocopying totals).

(30 marks)

OVER

QUESTION 2

Situation: You are Office Manager of a small British company. Your Director has heard about the 'Fax' service which is now available and has sent you some questions about it.

Task: Look at the Director's questions below. Answer these questions using the information from the Reprofax brochure below.

Note: Your answers need not be written in full sentences - numbers or short answers are acceptable where appropriate. Your answers should be as helpful as possible.

Example: Can I find out more about the Reprofax service?

Answer: Yes. Call in at the local office, or phone the local office, or dial 100 and ask for Freefone Reprofax.

1   What does 'Fax' mean?
2   How does Fax transmit messages?
3   Is Fax charged like a telegram (i.e. so much per word)?
4   Is Fax available only in the UK?
5   How can we receive a Fax message if we don't have a Fax machine in the office?
6   How long does it take to transmit a document by Fax?
7   Must all documents be printed or typed?
8   Can we send documents such as maps and diagrams by Fax?
9   Do all kinds of document cost the same amount to send by Fax
10   How can we send a Fax message if
     (a)   we **don't** have a Fax machine, but
     (b)   our client **does** have a Fax machine?

11   How can we send a Fax message if
     (a)   we **don't** have a Fax machine, and
     (b)   our client **doesn't** have a Fax machine?

12   How can we send a Fax message if
     (a)   we **do** have a Fax machine, and
     (b)   our client also **does** have a Fax machine?

13   How can we send a document by Fax if
     (a)   it is larger than A4 and
     (b)   the print is small?

(30 marks)

REPROFAX - High Speed 'Post' By Telephone

Reprofax Offices now provide a copying service (Fax), so that you can 'post' pages of text and graphics by telephone to almost anywhere in the UK and around the world in **minutes** rather than **days**.

All you do is call in to your nearest Reprofax Office and ask for your documents to be sent by Fax. They can be sent to another Reprofax Office or to anyone who owns a Fax machine. We can also deliver the 'fax' to any address within 50 kilometres (35 miles) of a Reprofax Office (at an extra charge) if the addressees can't call in and collect it themselves.

You can send as many A4 (30cm x 21cm/11$\frac{3}{4}$ in x 8$\frac{1}{4}$in) pages as you like and it doesn't matter how much information they contain because you pay only by the **page** and **not** by the word. Nor does it matter what **type** of information you send - Fax machines can transmit all kinds of information (handwritten, typed, printed or drawn) with equal speed, ease and cost.

So you can send quick handwritten messages, urgent letters or orders, important reports, plans, maps, diagrams - the list is almost endless.

You can also use our instant reduction and enlargement facilities to make larger documents fit onto A4 pages or to clarify small print or fine detail that is difficult to read.

And if you've **already** got a facsimile machine in your office, you can use the Reprofax network as a quick and convenient means of 'posting' information to clients who don't possess one.

For more information about our facsimile service, call in to or telephone your nearest Reprofax Office, or dial 100 and ask for Freefone Reprofax.

QUESTION 3

Situation: You work for a large company based in Manchester in the north of England. The company has just installed a new telephone system. The instructions for the new system are given on the next page.

Task: The new system comes into operation today. Here are some of the numbers you need to know and some of the people you have to call today. **Give the numbers you will have to dial.**

1   The company switchboard.
2   Directory Enquiries.
3   The International Operator.
4   The company security office.
5   The police.
6   Mr Richards, the accountant in room 43 on the 4th floor.
7   Mrs Oakes, the Personnel Manager in room 7 on floor 8.
8   Miss Rogers in reception (room 1 on the ground floor).
9   Homewood Ltd, a local company. Their number is Manchester 339 7600.
10   Your own home in Manchester - number 998 4144.
11   A local company. The number on their letterhead is 061-761 6167.
12   The Oxford branch of your company on Oxford 517693.
13   A supplier in London whose number is 587 8245

14   A company representative who called to see you last week. The number on his business card is 0703-81694.

15   Your Hungarian office in Budapest (area code 1), whose local number is 47391.

16   A customer in the USA on Chicago (312) 280850.
17   A client in Colchester in south-east England. His number is Colchester 592761.

18   Your company's agent in Zambia, whose number is Kitwe (area code 2) 66925.

(20 marks)

INSTRUCTIONS FOR NEW TELEPHONE SYSTEM

INTERNAL COMPANY CALLS

Dial floor number 0-8	Followed by room number 01-99*

*rooms numbered 1-9 have phone numbers 01-09
(In case of difficulty, dial the Switchboard - 123)

LOCAL NUMBERS WITHIN MANCHESTER

Dial 9 for an outside line	Followed by customer's number*

*To call a Manchester number beginning 061-: omit the area code (061) and dial only the figures after the hyphen

INLAND CALLS WITHIN THE UNITED KINGDOM

Dial 9 for an outside line	Followed by the area code*	Followed by customer's number

*Aberdeen	0224	Leeds	0532	Plymouth	0752
Birmingham	021	Liverpool	051	Portsmouth	0705
Bristol	0272	London (central)	071	Reading	0734
Cambridge	0223	Manchester	061	Sheffield	0742
Cardiff	0222	Newcastle	091	Southampton	0703
Edinburgh	031	Nottingham	0602	York	0904
Glasgow	041	Oxford	0865		

(For other area codes, see your telephone directory or call Directory Enquiries on 192)

INTERNATIONAL CALLS

Dial 9 for an outside line	Dial the International code 010	Followed by the country code*	Followed by the area code	Followed by customer's number

Country	Code	Country	Code	Country	Code
*Argentina	54	Germany(West)	49	Philippines	63
Australia	61	Greece	30	Poland	48
Austria	43	Hungary	36	Romania	40
Belgium	32	India	91	Singapore	65
Brazil	55	Indonesia	62	South Africa	27
Burma	95	Iran	98	Spain	34
Canada	1	Italy	39	Sri Lanka	94
Chile	56	Japan	81	Sweden	46
China	86	Korea	82	Switzerland	41
Colombia	57	Malaysia	60	Thailand	66
Cuba	53	Mexico	52	Turkey	90
Czechoslovakia	42	Netherlands	31	USA	1
Denmark	45	New Zealand	64	USSR	7
Egypt	20	Norway	47	Venezuela	58
France	33	Pakistan	92	Yugoslavia	38
Germany (East)	37	Peru	51		

For other countries call the International Operator on 108

EMERGENCIES
Company Security: 111
Fire/Police/Ambulance: 9-999

QUESTION 4

Situation: This situation continues from question 2.

The local Reprofax office has provided details of its 'Fax' service. As Office Manager in the UK you are interested in this service.

Task: Use the information from the Reprofax brochure below to complete the table of charges below. You should complete the following lines:

Lines 1-5

Lines (a), (b) and (c)

Lines (i) and (ii)

Note: Copy the table into your answer booklet. Write your answers in your answer booklet. Do not write on this question paper.

(20 marks)

HOW MUCH DOES FAX COST?

Transmission charges for the Fax service vary according to the number of pages and the distance.

Prices below show the cost of sending the **first** A4 (30cm x 21cm/11® in x 8´in) page. For each **additional page** the cost is reduced by half.

There are five area zones:

Zone 1 - **Local** (within 50 kilometres/35 miles) ....£4 for the first A4 page.
Zone 2 - **Rest of UK** ....£5 for the first A4 page.
Zone 3 - **Rest of Europe** ....£6 for the first A4 page.
Zone 4 - **North America** ....£7 for the first A4 page.
Zone 5 - **Rest of the World** ....£8 for the first A4 page.

Handling charges:

(a)   From one Reprofax office to another - no handling charge.
(b)   From a customer's Fax Machine to a Reprofax office - £3 handling charge (no additional charge for additional pages).
(c)   From a Reprofax office to a customer's Fax machine - no handling charge.

Reduction/enlargement:

(i)   Reduction from a larger paper to A4 paper suitable for Fax transmission - £1 per page.
(ii)   Enlargement from A4 in order to clarify print and fine detail - £2 per page.

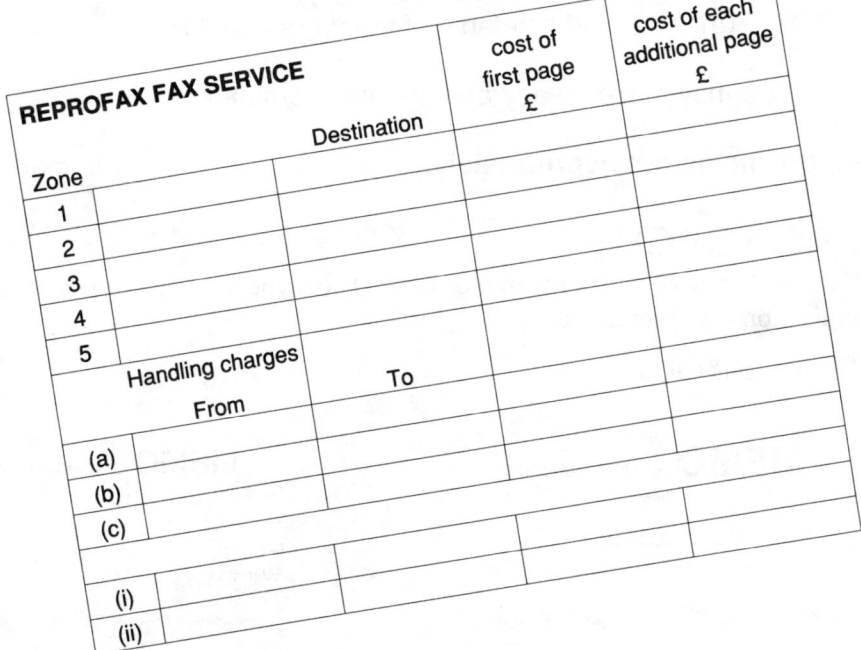

QUESTION 1

1 SAMPLE QUESTION

Situation: In about four months' time your company will hold its annual one-day sales conference in the capital city of your country. All sales staff from regional offices will attend. You have attended several planning meetings for this conference and you know all the details that have been decided so far. You also know that, after the Sales Manager's opening speech, information about new products will be given, followed by regional sales reports in the afternoon.

Task: Write a **memo**, on behalf of the Sales Manager, to all Sales Staff, giving preliminary information about the sales conference. Make sure that you include information about:

      (a)   date
      (b)   time
      (c)   place
      (d)   transport arrangements
      (e)   arrangements for meals and accommodation
      (f)   reception details
      (g)   a brief timetable of the day's events

Note: You may make up any appropriate information.

Set the memo out appropriately.   (30 marks)

2 APPROACH

Question 1 may be either a memo or letter. The layouts of these types of communication are quite different.

MEMO LAYOUT

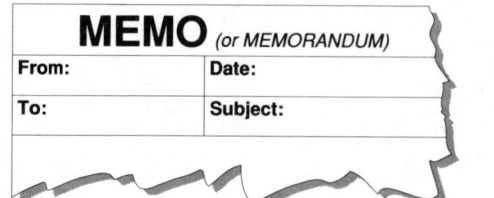

WRITING THE MEMO

1   Check whether the question asks you to write as yourself (in which case you can use your own name), or *on behalf of* someone else, using their name. The *From* section can be completed in various ways:

> **From:**   AJK
> **From:**   A J Kenning
> **From:**   A J Kenning, Accounts Manager

2   The memo may be to a person, identified by name or job title (or both) or to a group of people:

> **To:**   BWS
> **To:**   Mrs B W Shephard
> **To:**   Mrs B W Shephard, Office Manager
> **To:**   Office Manager
> **To:**   All Office Staff

3   The date will normally be the date of the examination unless there is something in the question indicating a different date.

4   Before you write your final answer, make a note on rough paper of the points to make in the memo. The sample question invites you to 'make up any appropriate information'. Do this first. Then group the points logically into paragraphs, and arrange them in the best order. Three to six paragraphs are usually appropriate: the memo should not be one long paragraph, nor should there be one paragraph for every little point. In some cases - especially if describing procedures or giving instructions - it can be helpful to number the paragraphs.

5   The style should be businesslike, which means neither too formal nor too informal. Aim for a neutral style, for example:
'Our driver will call at your hotel at 8 am and take you to the new factory'
rather than:
'Our chauffeur will be in attendance at eight to convey your good self to our premises' (too formal)
or:
'One of our guys will pick you up at eight sharp, if that's OK' (too informal).

6   You should not sign a memo, but you may put initials at the end.

7   After writing, check through the memo carefully for mistakes in grammar, spelling, or punctuation. If you are not sure, change it to something which you *know* is correct.

LETTER LAYOUT

ALPHA INTERNATIONAL LINKS LTD
23 Wentworth Place, Colchester, Essex CO1 3DL

Alternative positions for sender's company and address

ALPHA INTERNATIONAL LINKS LTD
23 Wentworth Place
Colchester
Essex
CO1 3DL

14 November 1991   **Alternative:** 14th November 1991
                         Alternative position   14 November 1991

Mr A Varney   Addressee's name and title, company and address.
Operations Manager   Note: It is very common, acceptable practice to omit full
Betamix Concretes Ltd   stops (.) after **Mr** and **Ltd,** and to omit commas (,) at the
Peterborough Road   end of each line of the address. If full stops and commas
Weston   are used, they must be used consistently.
Northants
NN8 6FS

Dear Mr Varney   The subject line is underlined (no **Subject** or **Re**)
Revised Construction Schedule

Thank you for ...   Note: the paragraph begins at the left margin.

Yours sincerely   - If you know the name of the person you are writing to:
                           Dear Mr Varney + **Yours sincerely**
                         - If you do not know the name of the person you are writing
                           to: **Dear Sir or Madam** + **Yours faithfully**
                         - If you are writing to the company for the first time and have
                           had no previous contact with the company: **Dear Sirs**+
                           Yours faithfully (By writing **Dear Sirs** you are addressing
                           all the directors of the company).

SVance

S Vance (Mr)   or **(Mrs)** or **(Dr)** or **(Ms)**
Purchasing Director   Job title is underlined

Enc.   = enclosures. Sometimes these are named, e.g.: **Enc. brochure.**

WRITING THE LETTER

1   As with the memo, first list on rough paper the points which you want to make
    in the letter, inventing where necessary. Put them in logical order, and see which
    ones are linked and can therefore be put together in paragraphs.
    Many letters have this structure:

    • First paragraph gives the reason for writing.

    • Central paragraphs contain the key messages of the letter.

    • Last paragraph gives the next step (eg suggesting meeting, telephone call etc).

2   The style of the letter is important, as this can affect the image of the company.
    Some candidates try to appear businesslike by writing in a very cold and formal
    way. However, in English business letters, writers try to convey the same tone
    as in face-to-face conversations. Before writing, ask yourself whether, judging
    from the situation, the letter should be friendly or formal. If it should be friendly,
    do not hesitate to express thanks (I was very pleased to receive your letter…),
    enthusiasm (I very much enjoyed our meeting recently), or optimism (I very
    much look forward to…).

3   As always, check your letter afterwards, for:

    (a) Layout, as explained above

    (b) The appropriate tone

    (c) Language correctness. If there is anything about which you are not certain,
        rewrite it using English which you *know* is correct.

3 MODEL ANSWER

From: Sales Manager

To: Regional Sales Staff

Date: 14 May 1991

Subject: Annual Sales Conference

This year's Sales Conference will take place on Thursday, 12 September at the Tudor Gate Hotel, 1 Princes Way, London SW7 4QJ (tel. 01 778 9388). All sales staff from regional offices will attend. Since the conference will begin at 9 am, staff will travel to London after lunch on Wednesday, 11 September. The company is making special arrangements for travel by coach and train and details for these will be sent to you nearer the time.

Staff will be booked into the Tudor Gate Hotel for two nights, 11 and 12 September, and will return home on the morning of 13 September. All meals will be provided at the hotel from dinner on Wednesday evening to breakfast on Friday morning. On arrival, staff should collect their identity badges and conference folders from the special reception desk in the hotel foyer. Please wear your identity badge at all times.

It is expected that the conference timetable will be as follows:

9.00	Sales Manager's Opening Speech
9.30	New Product Information
10.30	Coffee Break
10.45	New Product Information
12.30	Lunch
2.00	Regional Sales Reports
3.30	Tea
3.45	Regional Sales Reports
5.30	End of Conference

You will receive further information when all the details have been finalized.

4 COMMENTS ON MODEL ANSWER

LAYOUT (5 marks)

This answer would receive full marks for layout, since there is nothing missing, and it is clear, accurate and easy to understand. These marks are for the layout at the top of the memo. The timetable has been marked under Content.

CONTENT (15 marks)

Fullness

This memo covers all the seven points that are mentioned in the question:

- date of conference
- time of conference
- location of conference
- transport arrangements
- meals and accommodation
- reception details
- conference timetable.

Relevance

The writer has realised from certain phrases in the question ('details that have been decided so far', 'preliminary information') that the purpose of the memo is to give initial information to staff well in advance so that they can avoid arranging their own meetings and visits during the time of the conference. It is not therefore necessary to give detailed information about transport now. It is enough to indicate that the company will arrange this, and that more details will follow.

Accuracy

The writer has realised that the conference is for one day but that staff will need to stay one or two nights because of the travelling time involved. England has been taken as the example here, but in a larger country staff might need to stay longer and in a small country it might be possible to avoid an overnight stay. Candidates are expected to take account of local conditions. This also applies to the starting and finishing time of the conference, and to the meal breaks. In this case the writer has chosen times that are reasonable for British circumstances.

The writer has noted from the question that the conference is 'in about four months' time.' Therefore, the date of the memo is the date of the exam and the conference date is about four months ahead of that date.

Creativity

The writer has made up appropriate details that are not mentioned in the question. Apart from the date, name of hotel and so on, these include a reference to the importance of wearing identity badges. Good answers to this question cover all the points in the question and include realistic and relevant invented information.

LANGUAGE (10 marks)

Mechanical accuracy

This answer is free of errors of punctuation, spelling and grammar and no marks would be deducted for such errors.

Appropriate style

The style is formal, but not too much so. It is written in clear and direct style and does its job of conveying information effectively.

This answer is certainly at Distinction level.

5 SECOND ANSWER

from: Sales Manager

TO: Sales Staff   4/5/

Conference we are going to have in capital city of your country

Dear Employees,

We are going to have Sales Conference next month. You all have to come. It will be at Tudor Gate Hotel in London, and you will stay there for two nights, all meals included. You don't have to pay. It has been brought to my attention that some of you didn't wear your identity badges at our last conference. Please make sure you do so this time

1 Sales Manager's Opening Speech
2 Information about new products
3 Lunch
4 Regonal Sales Reports
5 Finish

I hope we have a really successful conference and I am looking forward to meet you all again.

If you have any querris, please do not hesitate to contact me, or give Sue a ring, she deals with enquiries.

Yours Sincerely

Rod Random
Sales Manager

6 COMMENTS ON SECOND ANSWER

LAYOUT (5 marks)

The writer confuses memo layout with letter layout. The date is given in a very inadequate way and capitals and small letters are used inconsistently. The subject is just copied from the question. The writer begins and ends the memo as if it were a letter, but even the letter layout is not correct - 'sincerely' should have a small 's' for example.

This answer would receive, at the most, 2 marks for language.

CONTENT (15 marks)

Fullness

The writer attempts to cover
- place
- meals
- reception arrangements
- conference timetable

but completely omits
- date
- time
- travel arrangements.

He does not give the full address of the hotel or any details of the meals and the conference timetable is very inadequate. We are invited to 'phone Sue' but her number is not given. He has not used the information in the question to advantage.

Relevance

The writer has not picked up the indications in the question that things have not been finalized and this aspect does not appear in his answer. He has ignored the phrase 'In about four months' time' and said that the conference is next month. He has not considered the relevance of the information to the people who are receiving the message.

Accuracy

This answer lacks precise and consistent details of times and dates. The numbering (although sometimes appropriate in memos) conveys no useful information.

Creativity

Despite the reference to identity badges, the writer has not invented points of his own which fit in realistically with the points given in the question. There is little awareness that there is a creative aspect to this question.

No more than 5 marks could be given for content.

LANGUAGE (10 marks)

Mechanical accuracy

Capital and small letters are used inconsistently. Although the word *regional* occurs in the question it is spelt wrongly, as is *queries*. There are several grammar errors:

> to have (a) sales conference
> look forward to meet(ing) you
> give Sue a ring, she deals with enquiries.

3

3 marks would be lost here.

Appropriate style

The answer is very weak here. It includes formal phrases such as 'It has been brought to my notice' and 'Please do not hesitate to contact me' with very colloquial, conversational phrases such as 'You all have to come', and 'give Sue a ring'.

3 marks would be lost here, leaving a total of 4 marks for language.

7 SUMMARY OF COMMON ERRORS

LAYOUT
- Confusion of letter and memo formats.
- Incorrect use of either format.

CONTENT
- Failure to understand the real reason for the communication.
- Uncertainty of the relationship between sender and receiver.
- Omission of key points of content.
- Poor grouping and ordering of points into paragraphs.
- Lack of distinction between major and minor points.
- Inappropriate treatment of time and distance.

STYLE
- Too formal or informal in style for the situation.
- Inconsistency of style in the same letter or memo.

LANGUAGE
- Spelling mistakes, especially where the misspelt word appears on the question paper.
- Grammatical errors, especially relatives (*which*), articles (*a, the*), participles (*taking, taken*), and sentence construction (joining two sentences ungrammatically, without a conjunction).

8 FURTHER PRACTICE

Situation: You work for a company that manufactures safety equipment, such as life
              rafts, for use on small boats. You have received an enquiry about your
              products from a French retailer. Your sales manager, Mrs Joanna
              MacDonald, has asked you to write a reply for her signature.

Task: Write a reply to the letter, including the information in Mrs MacDonald's notes
              opposite.

Méridien S.A.

2 quai de Grenelle, 13269 MARSEILLE, France

Tél. 91.76.41.21

Télex 440 557

```
Champion Manufacturing plc
1 Horseferry Road
PORTSMOUTH
PO12 3RT
United Kingdom                              20 November 19-
```

Dear Sirs

We have seen advertisements in the British trade press for the
'Bounty' life raft, which is manufactured by your company.

We supply a wide range of goods, including safety equipment,
to the owners of leisure craft and fishing boats based in the
South of France and we are interested in receiving further
information about the 'Bounty' life raft.

We would like to know if this product is available for export
and, if so, to have details of your trade and quantity
discounts.

We look forward to hearing from you.

Yours faithfully

Pierre Imbernon

Pierre Imbernon
Commercial Manager

Mrs MacDonald's notes -

Send brochure with full technical details - in French - and video-cassette (French version) + price list for different models (send video separately). Discounts - only 10% off list price unless more than 100 are ordered. Write today - mention the 'Salon Nautique International de Paris' (International Paris Boat Show) 30 November - 10 December, at Porte de Versailles - all our products will be exhibited there, including the 'Bounty'.

Paul Martin is already in Paris (I've already phoned him about this) and will contact Mr Imbernon.

(30 marks)

MARKING SCHEME

Content

Acknowledge receipt of letter and express appreciation of enquiry	1
Refer to excellence of product	2
Confirm that it is for export	2
Enclosed brochure and price-list	2
Say that video film has been sent separately	2
Refer to Paris Boat Show	2
Mention Paul Martin (identify him as the Chief Salesman)	2
Say that Paul Martin will be in contact - by phone	2
	15

Language

Mechanical accuracy - deduct half mark for each error	7
Appropriate style for letter	3
	10

Layout

Appropriate date	1
Sender's name and address	1
Recipient's name and address	1
Dear Mr Imbernon	1
Yours sincerely + name + position	1
This information must be in the correct position	5
	30

QUESTION 2

I SAMPLE QUESTION

Situation: Your company sends a large amount of mail overseas. Your Office Manager has heard of the SWIFTAIR service and has asked you to find out more about it. You have obtained an information leaflet.

Task: Look at the Office Manager's questions below. Answer these questions using information from the leaflet. Your answers need not be in full sentences - numbers or short answers are acceptable where appropriate. Your answers should be as helpful as possible.

Example: How much does one C4 Swiftpack cost?

Answer: £2.00

1 Do Swiftair items go separately from the normal mail?

2 What is the weight limit for letters?

3 Are Swiftair items always put on an aeroplane on the day they are posted?

4 What is the extra charge for SWIFTAIR items?

5 Can Swiftpacks be sent to all countries?

6 How do the post office workers recognise Swiftair items?

7 When do I have to use a C2/CP3 form?

8 Is it better to buy a pack of ten C4 Swiftpacks than to buy ten one by one at the post office?

9 Where are Swiftair items sorted?

10 Will the Post Office collect Swiftair items from my office?

11 Can I obtain a large quantity of Swiftpacks?

12 How can I obtain a large quantity of Swiftpacks?

13 What is the main advantage of Swiftair compared with a courier service?

14 Does the Post Office guarantee delivery within a certain period?

15 If you use a Swiftpack, do you have to put stamps on it?

(30 marks)

SWIFTAIR

ROYAL MAIL INTERNATIONAL LETTERS

When you need to send important mail abroad *SWIFTAIR* is the express airmail service that ensures that your letters, papers, or documents will arrive safely and economically.

HERE'S HOW IT WORKS

SWIFTAIR is a priority letter service from the Royal Mail, which means that it has access to a vast international network of postal collection and delivery channels. This means that *SWIFTAIR* items travel with the normal mail but at each handling point *SWIFTAIR* mail receives special treatment, speeding its sorting and onward despatch.

On arrival at one of our four international sorting offices, *SWIFTAIR* items are immediately transferred and separately processed. They are then expressed to their destination on the first available flight, even on the day of posting, whenever possible.

ECONOMY

Because *SWIFTAIR* mail travels within the international postal network it does not incur the high delivery costs of an expensive courier service. In this way *SWIFTAIR* provides an economical - as well as effective - alternative for all those times when you don't need a guaranteed ultra high speed delivery.

SIMPLICITY

Just take your letter or packet to the Post Office, add stamps to the value of the normal airmail postage plus £1.65, then affix the red SWIFTAIR express label and leave the rest to us. If you have a regular collection at your office, simply include your SWIFTAIR item in that. Alternatively if the mail you are sending fits in a standard DL (10cm x 21.5cm), C5 (16.5cm x 23cm) or C4 (23cm x 33cm) envelope why not use one of our *SWIFTPACKS*?

SWIFTPACKS

SWIFTPACKS are a completely pre-paid envelope for items up to 60gms in weight and can be sent anywhere in the world. You can purchase them singly at your post office counter or by mail order from the address shown in this leaflet.

ADDITIONAL BENEFITS

Whether you use the *SWIFTAIR* service or convenient SWIFTPACKS you can register or insure your *SWIFTAIR* items to most countries and a certificate of posting is available, free of charge, on request.

MERCHANDISE

When sending merchandise by *SWIFTAIR* all items must carry the green douane C1 label. If the value of the merchandise is over £270 then a C2/CP3 form must be used.

WEIGHT LIMITS

Small Packets	1Kg
Letters or Printed Papers	2Kg
Certain Books and Pamphlets	5Kg

SWIFTPACK PRICES

SWIFTPACKS are available in 3 sizes from your local post office at the following prices:

DL (10cm x 21.5cm)	£1.90
C5 (16.5cm x 23cm)	£1.95
C4 (23cm x 33cm)	£2.00

and don't forget, that is fully pre-paid to anywhere in the world for 60gms weight.

MAIL ORDER SERVICE

If you require a stock of SWIFTPACKS they are available in packs of 10, 15, or 25. Just send your cheque, made payable to 'The Post Office' with your order to:

Swiftpacks
Freepost
The Publicity Centre
Fenton Way
Basildon
Essex SS15 4BR
(NO STAMP REQUIRED)

MAIL ORDER PRICES

	10	15	25
DL	£19.00	£27.75	£45.00
C5	£19.50	£28.50	£46.00
C4	£20.00	£29.00	£47.00

SWIFTAIR is a priority letter service NOT a guaranteed courier service.

2 APPROACH

Question 2 consists of a short prose passage, usually authentic, on a topic of practical interest to business people.

QUESTION TYPES

Various types of question may be found here.

Open-ended questions with short answers

Question

How much does the hotel charge for one night?

Answer

£40 single, £60 double

Multiple choice questions

Question

1   The British Airways leaflet is

a   an advertisement

b   an article in a business magazine

c   information material

Answer

1c

Other types of comprehension questions, such as TRUE/FALSE, may also be used.

FINDING THE ANSWERS

Look at the questions first in order to get an approximate idea of what information you need to find in the passage. However, remember that the questions will not be in the same order as the information in the passage and it is therefore important to *read the whole passage* before you begin to answer the questions. When you look at the passage again, you should search for the specific piece of information you need to answer the question. Looking through the passage to find specific information is called *scanning*.

FULL ANSWERS ?

There is no need to copy out the question. Just put the number followed by your answer. If the questions are open-ended, you may answer with a short sentence, a phrase, or a single word or a number, whichever is most appropriate. Make sure that you give a *full* answer. For example, if the question is

Can I make international calls from my room?

it is better to answer

No, you have to go through the operator

than to answer simply *No*.

Sometimes there may be two pieces of information in one answer and this information may appear in different places in the passage. You will have to combine this information in your answer.

Provided your answer is intelligible you will get a mark, but do your best to avoid mistakes in grammar, spelling, and punctuation.

3 MODEL ANSWER (2 marks for each correct answer)

1   No, they go with the normal mail.
2   2Kg.
3   No, only whenever possible.
4   £1.65.
5   Yes, they can.
6   By the red labels.
7   When the value of your merchandise is over £270.
8   It doesn't make any difference – the price is the same.
9   At one of four international sorting offices.
10 Only if you already have a regular collection.
11 Yes, if you ask for one.
12 By mail order.
13 It is much cheaper.
14 No, it doesn't.
15 No, you don't.

4 COMMENTS ON MODEL ANSWER

The model answer illustrates various ways of expressing the correct information:

- a short sentence (answer 13)
- a word or number (answer 2)
- a phrase (answer 12)
- a negative or positive answer with a brief explanation (answer 3)
- a negative or positive answer (answer 14).

Another good feature of this answer is that it uses the words and phrases from the passage but does not copy out lengthy and irrelevant passages.

The answers are clearly numbered.

It is better to write the answers vertically down the page and there is plenty of room in the answer book to do this.

For some questions, (8 for example) information from different parts of the passage has been used to reach the correct answer.

This answer would receive full marks.

5 SECOND ANSWER

1 Do SWIFTAIR items go separately from the normal mail?

SWIFTAIR items travel with the normal mail but at each handling point SWIFTAIR mail receives special treatment, speeding its sorting and onward despatch.

2 What is the weight limit for letters?

The weight limit for letter is 1Kg.

3 They are then expressed to their destination on the first available flight, even on the day of posting, whenever possible.

4 £1.90   5 Anywhere 6 express labels   7 merchandise of £270

8 It is cheaper to buy in bulk. 9 Four international sorting offices

10 Yes   11   Yes

12 If you require a stock of SWIFTPACKS they are available in packs of 10, 15 or 25. Just send your cheque, made payable to "The Post Office" with your order to:-

SWIFTPACKS
FREEPOST
the Publicity Centre, Fenton Way,
Basildon, Essex SS15 4BR

(NO STAMP REQUIRED)

13 SWIFTAIR is a priority letter service NOT a guaranteed courier service.

14 The Post Office ensures that your letters, papers or documents will arrive safely and economically.

15 Add stamps to the value of the normal airmail postage plus £1.65.

6 COMMENTS ON SECOND ANSWER

- The writer has begun by writing out the question in full, which is not necessary.
- Answer 2 shows an example of carelessness - *letter* instead of *letters*.
- Answer 3 is an undigested chunk from the passage.
- Some of the answers are written horizontally across the page, which makes them more difficult to mark.
- In answer 4 the writer has confused Swiftair items with Swiftpack prices.
- Answers 5, 6 and 7 are short but simply do not convey enough accurate information.
- In answer 8, the writer is relying on his knowledge of the world, not on what it says in the passage. It is normally cheaper to buy in bulk, but in this case you need to buy more than ten to save money.
- Answer 9 contains accurate information but the vital preposition , *At*, which ties it to the question, is missing.
- Answers 10 and 11 miss out vital qualifying information.
- Several answers are copied at length directly from the passage. Even if such answers contain the correct answer to the question (as in 12) they would not receive all the marks available, since such an answer does not provide clear evidence of understanding.
- In many cases (13 and 14 for example) the quotation from the passage does not answer the question. It simply contains a word which also appears in the question.
- In answer 15, the writer has again confused Swiftair items with Swiftpacks.

This answer would receive no more than a third of the total marks for the question.

7 SUMMARY OF COMMON ERRORS

CONTENT

- Copying out the questions.
- Quoting long sections from the passage, instead of answering questions directly.
- Giving answers too short to be complete.
- Use of vague rather than precise information.
- Not linking relevant information from different parts of the passage to provide a full answer.

PRESENTATION

- Numbering questions wrongly.
- Listing questions horizontally across the page, which can create confusion, or compressing answers into a very small corner of a page.

ACCURACY

- Misspelling of words given in the passage. Spelling is not normally penalized in this question, except where the word is already given on the question paper.

8 FURTHER PRACTICE

Situation: The company for which you work is planning to increase its exports to Germany. You were asked to find out as much information as possible about one part of Germany - Schleswig-Holstein - in preparation for a meeting.

Task: At the meeting, several comments were made about Schleswig-Holstein. Some were partly true, and some were inaccurate. You responded to these comments by adding more information to the ones that were partly true and correcting the ones that were wrong. Using the information in the passage below, write down what you said. Your answer should be in the form of short phrases and sentences.

Example: Schleswig-Holstein has an area of 15,000 square miles, doesn't it?

No, it's 15,710 square kilometres, to be exact.

1   Lubeck is the capital of Schleswig-Holstein, isn't it?

2   There's a big river in the south of this area, isn't there?

3   I've heard it's a good place for mountain-climbing.

4   I hear there are going to be some job losses.

5   About three million people live there.

6   It's not a very nice place to spend a holiday.

7   Agriculture is a very important economic activity.

8   Most of the farmers grow wheat and sugar beet.

9   There's quite a lot of inshore fishing.

10   It has a long coastline along the Baltic Sea, doesn't it?

11   None of the towns has more than 50,000 inhabitants.

12   Vegetables and fruits are grown mainly in the south-east.

13   The western part of Schleswig-Holstein has a border with Denmark.

14   Agricultural productivity is greater here than in most parts of Germany.

15   More than 17 million people visited the area in 1986.

(30 marks)

Schleswig-Holstein

The province reaches from the border with Denmark in the north to the river Elbe in the south; it includes all of the West German coastline on the Baltic sea and a large part of its North Sea coastline. It is extremely flat with relatively little forest, the predominant land use being agricultural. It has an area of 15,710 square kilometres and a population of 2.612 million (30 April 1987).

Agricultural productivity is almost three times the West German average in terms of the GDP (4.6 per cent against 1.7 per cent in 1985). The main emphasis lies on livestock breeding (dairy and beef cattle). Arable crops like wheat and sugar beet are found in the south-east of Schleswig-Holstein. The world's biggest nursery area is situated near Pinneberg. Field vegetables and fruits are extensively grown in western Schleswig-Holstein. However, important though agriculture is to the area, it accounts for a declining share of its GDP. Schleswig-Holstein maintains a small-scale deep-sea fishing fleet, together with some inshore fishing. Industries like shipbuilding, mechanical engineering and metal manufacturing are concentrated in the major towns. Almost 33 per cent of the North German shipbuilding industry's labour force is employed in Schleswig-Holstein. During 1987, about 4,000 (out of 12,500) jobs are to be cut due to the likely closure of three major shipyards. The sea-side resorts at the coasts are completely devoted to tourism: during 1986 well over 17 million overnight stays were registered. Kiel (population 244,046) is the capital and Lubeck is the other principal town (210,300), but there are several small towns of between 20-50,000.

MARKING SCHEME AND ANSWERS

2 marks per correct answer. 1 mark if it is partly correct.

1 No, Kiel is the capital.

2 Yes, the river Elbe.

3 No, it's extremely flat.

4 Yes, about 4,000 jobs are likely to be cut.

5 The population is 2.612 million, to be precise.

6 Yes, it is. The seaside resorts are devoted to tourism.

7 Yes, but it is declining relative to other industries.

8 No, most of them keep dairy and beef cattle.

9 Yes, but there is deep-sea fishing as well.

10 Yes, and on the North Sea as well.

11 Not true. Kiel has 244,046 and Lubeck 210,300.

12 No, they are grown in the west.

13 No, the northern part borders Denmark.

14 Yes, it is 4.6% of GDP as against an average of 1.7 for West Germany as a whole.

15 No, there were more than 17 million overnight stays, which isn't the same thing.

QUESTION 3

I SAMPLE QUESTION

Situation: You work for a company which builds houses for sale and your manager has asked you to collect some information about how many houses in Britain are owned by the people living in them and how many are rented, and how this has changed since the beginning of the twentieth century.

Task: Study the three pie charts carefully and use the information in them to complete the gaps in the sentences below. Use **one** word or date in each gap.

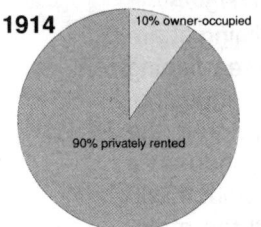
1914 — 10% owner-occupied, 90% privately rented

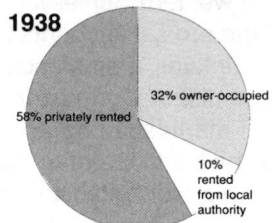
1938 — 32% owner-occupied, 58% privately rented, 10% rented from local authority

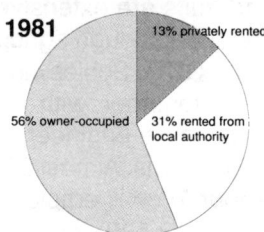
1981 — 13% privately rented, 56% owner-occupied, 31% rented from local authority

Since 1914, there has been a very big (1) . . . . in the proportion of houses that are owned by the people who live in them and a very big (2) . . . . in the proportion rented from private landlords.

In 1914 (3) . . . . houses were rented from local authorities, but by 1938 exactly one (4) . . . . .of houses were rented in this way and by 1981 the proportion had risen to just under one (5) . . . .

In 1938 just under a (6) . . . . .of all houses were owner-occupied, more than three (7).. . . . . more than in 1910, and by 1981 more than (8) . . . . of all houses were owned in this way.

The proportion of houses which were owner-occupied in 1938 is nearly the (9) . . . . as the proportion of houses rented from a local authority in 1981.

The decline in private renting was fastest between (10) . . . . .and (11). . . . . whereas the increase in owner-occupation was fastest between (12). . . . . and (13). . . . .

In 1914 almost (14). . . . . houses were privately rented but in 1981 very (15) . . . . were.

The proportion of owner-occupied houses in 1981 is nearly (16) . . . . .the figure for 1938.

In 1981 nearly (17) . . . . as many houses were owner-occupied as were rented from local authorities.

In 1938 a lot more than (18) . . . . .of all houses were rented.

In 1981 owner-occupation was the (19) . . . . common form of house occupation and private renting the (20) . . . . common.

(20 marks)

2 APPROACH

Question 3 requires only short answers, based on inputs of various kinds. These
may include:

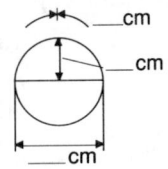

- pie charts (as opposite)

- tables   • flow charts   • histograms or bar charts

- graphs

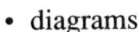

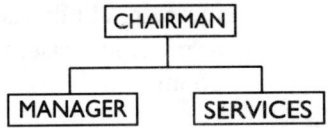

- building plans

- maps   • diagrams   • organization charts

From the information they give, you must complete a passage, usually by giving
only one or two words per question. The challenge lies in the correct interpretation
of the information.

PREPARATION

How can you prepare? The information could be on an almost infinite number of
subjects; however, there are certain areas of language which you can revise in order
to improve your chance of interpreting complex information correctly.

Percentages

If a firm's market share increases from 10% one year to 20% the next, that
represents a 100% increase.

Numbers and proportion

Terms such as a quarter, a fifth, three-quarters, and two-thirds often arise, as do
single, double, triple, twice, three times as many, and half as many. It is also
important to understand numbers both large (eg 57,003,224) and small (8.231).

Comparisons and superlatives

Common language in Question 3 includes:

more than, less than   the most, the least
better than, worse than   the best, the worst
higher than, lower than   the highest, the lowest
the same as

Expressions of quantity

much/many   none/some/any
little/few   all/every
a little/a few   hardly/fairly/rather/quite

Words which can be verbs, but also adjectives or nouns

Double:
Profits *doubled* last year (verb)
The price is *double* the competition's (adjective)
Average:
What is your *average* delivery period? (adjective)
What consumption do you *average*? (verb)
What is the margin, on an *average*? (noun)

Words expressing change in quantity

increase, climb, rise, upturn   decrease, drop, fall
to raise, increase, boom   to cut, reduce decrease
boom   decline

ANSWERING THE QUESTIONS

1 First, look at the visual information (the charts, graphs etc.) to be sure that you understand each chart individually *and* the relationship between the different charts.

2 Then, read through the Task quickly to get an overall impression of the questions. This quick read-through may show you that two or three questions are quite similar, and that you will need to be careful to give the precise answer to each of those questions.

3 One by one, go through the questions, numbering your answers as on the examination paper, laying them out vertically down the page. If you are *absolutely sure* of an answer, write it down; if not, leave that line empty and do the rest.

4 Return to the questions of which you are unsure. Instead of guessing, *test* possible answers to see whether they fit grammatically and with the information in the diagrams.

5 As a final step, check through your whole answer to the Task again. If you have used the same answer twice, this may be a mistake, as the same answer cannot often be used correctly for different questions.

3 MODEL ANSWER

1	increase
2	decrease
3	no
4	tenth
5	third
6	third
7	times
8	half
9	same
10	1938
11	1981
12	1910
13	1938
14	all
15	few
16	double
17	twice
18	half
19	most
20	least

4 COMMENTS ON MODEL ANSWER

- The answer is clearly set out, with the numbers vertically down the page and each answer next to its number, making the whole easy to read.
- The writer has obeyed the instruction to use only ONE word or date.
- She has fully understood the information in the pie charts and has also understood which type of word has to go in each gap. From the context, she has deduced that answers 1, 2, and 3 require lexical items, that 4, 5, and 6 require fractions, and that 10, 11, 12, and 13 require dates.
- She has fully digested the information in the pie charts and is able to reproduce it in a different form.
- In 1 and 2, *rise* and *fall* respectively would also be correct.

This answer would receive full marks.

5 SECOND ANSWER

1 *increased*   2 *decreased* 3 *any*

4 10%   5 *third*   6 *third*

7 *by*   8 *half*   9 *identical*

10 1910   11 1938   12 1938

13 1981 14 *every*   15 *a few*

16 60% 17 *double*   18 68%

19 56%   20 13%

6 COMMENTS ON SECOND ANSWER

- The writer has laid out the answers horizontally, which makes marking more difficult. However, he has not copied out the entire question, which many weaker candidates do.
- He has correctly answered 5, 6, and 8 and would therefore receive 3 marks for this question.
- In answers 1 and 2 he has got the right word but the wrong form of that word.
- Answer 3 indicates that he may not understand the difference between *none*, *some*, *nothing* and *anything*.
- In answer 4 the figure in the pie chart has been copied down without being changed to *tenth*.
- Answer 7 indicates that the writer is unsure how to use *times* and *by* in such expressions as 'three times three equals nine' and 'the room measures four metres by three metres'.
- In answer 9 *same* has been confused with *identical*.
- Answers 10, 11, 12, and 13 are wrong because the information in the pie charts has not been understood.
- Answer 14 indicates a confusion between *all* and *every*.
- In answer 15 the writer has disobeyed the instruction to use only ONE word, probably because he is not clear about the difference between *few* and *a few*.
- Answers 16 and 17 indicate confusion between *double* and *twice*.
- In answers 18, 19, and 20 the writer has simply copied from the pie chart the percentages that relate to the answer, without considering which words will fit correctly into the gaps.

7 SUMMARY OF COMMON ERRORS

- Untidy presentation of answers.
- Letters or numbers of questions missing, making it difficult to see what the answers refer to.
- Ignoring instructions about the number of words in the answer.
- Using the wrong form of a word - *decreasing* instead of *decreased*, for example.
- Inability to understand certain ways of displaying information.
- Inability to understand percentages or fractions.
- Using statistical information straight from the graphic or numerical material without changing it to fit the sentence - writing *50%* instead of *half* for example.
- Copying out the entire question.
- Using numbers instead of words or words instead of numbers.

8 FURTHER PRACTICE

Situation: You have to arrange rail and air travel for the sales representatives of the company that you work for. These representatives frequently ask you detailed questions about their travel arrangements.

Task: Using the information in the timetable, answer the following questions. Your answers will be in the form of short phrases, single words or times and numbers.

1   Is there a non-stop service from London to Sheffield?
2   What is the earliest time that I can arrive in Sheffield?
3   Are all the Monday-Friday trains InterCity services?
4   Is food available on all the morning Monday-Friday trains?
5   Which train to Sheffield provides the best meals service?
6   If I catch the 1300 train on Wednesday, when will I arrive in Sheffield?
7   I have got to be at a meeting in the centre of Sheffield on Tuesday at 2 pm. Which train do you advise me to take?
8   Can I reserve a seat on all train services to Sheffield?
9   If it says sx, does that train run on Saturday?
10   How can I find out information that doesn't appear on the timetable?
11   At what time does the 1000 service arrive in Sheffield on Thursday?
12   On what days can I leave London at 1725?
13   When is the last train to Sheffield on Sunday and when does it arrive?
14   Can I use a Saver ticket on a train that leaves London at 1700?
15   On which trains is it forbidden to use Saver tickets to travel to Sheffield?

INTERCITY

London → Sheffield
and Chesterfield

Principal train service 15 May to 1 October 1989

Mondays to Saturdays

	London St. Pancras depart		Chester-field arrive	Sheffield arrive
▲ ✖	0700	sx	0906	0922
●	0700	so	0906	0922
▲ ✖	0830		1034	1050
✖	1000		1207 b	1223 b
✖	1130		1333	1350
✖	1300		1505	1521
✖	1430		1634	1650
	1600		1810	1826
■ 🍴	1700	sx	1858	1914
	1700	so	1857	1914
■ ✖	1725	fsx	1947	2003
▼ ✖	1725	fo	1947	2003
✖	1800		2002	2017
✖	1900	sx	2110	2126
	1900	so	2113	2129
	1930	sx	2159	2215
	2000	sx	2218	2234
●	2100	so	2312	2328
	2200	sx	0015	0031
●	2300	sx	0125	0141
●	2300	so	0132	0148

Sundays

	London St. Pancras depart	Chester-field arrive	Sheffield arrive
●	0830	1119	1151
	1130	1401	1433
	1330	1602	1625
	1530	1752	1809
	1705	1920	1937
	1805	2019	2036
	1905	2124	2141
●	1935	2212	2228
●	2005	2233	2250
●	2105	2323	2339
●	2305	0157	0214

Notes

b	2 minutes earlier on Mondays to Fridays
fo	Fridays only
fsx	Fridays and Saturdays excepted
so	Saturdays only
sx	Saturdays excepted

All services shown in this timetable are InterCity unless otherwise stated. InterCity services offer First Class and Standard accommodation, light foc and hot and cold drinks and reserved seats.

🍴 InterCity Pullman train with full meal service to customers travelling First Class

✖ Service of meals including hot food to customers travelling First Class (and Standard, provided accommodation is available) on Mondays to Fridays

▲ OUTWARD portions of SAVER tickets are NOT valid on this train Mondays to Fridays

▼ RETURN portions of SAVER tickets are NOT valid on this train

■ SAVERS are NOT valid on this train

● NOT an InterCity service

Refreshments are available for all or part of the journey. Pullman and some other facilities may be withdrawn on Bank Holidays

For further information on train services, fares and other facilities, please telephone **London 01-387-7070**

The British Railways Board accept no liability for any inaccuracy in the information contained in this timetable - which is subject to alteration especially during Bank Holiday periods.

QUESTION 4

I SAMPLE QUESTION

Situation: Your company is about to open a Health and Fitness Centre on company premises for the use of staff and their families and friends. The opening times and other matters concerning the use of the centre were decided at a meeting of the Social and Welfare committee, the minutes of which are given below.

Task: Summarize the information in the minutes by completing the table below. This table is to be displayed on the staff notice-board so that staff can see at a glance what activities are available, when they are available, and for whom they are available.

Note: Give your answers in the following form:

1   open to all

2   weight-training, yoga, karate

(these are not necessarily correct)

and so on until 20.

Minutes of the Social and Welfare Committee:

...it was therefore agreed that all early morning sessions will be open to staff, their families and friends, with the exception of the Friday session which is for female staff only. Weight-training facilities will be available at this time, and at every other time. In addition, it will be possible to play table tennis and snooker every morning. All lunch-time sessions will be for staff only, with Wednesday reserved for female staff. There will be an aerobics class every lunchtime session except Tuesday, when the activities available will be the same throughout the day. The third lunchtime activity will be yoga from Wednesday to Friday and karate on Monday (also evening). Evening sessions will be open to all except for Wednesday which is for staff only and Thursday which is for female staff only. Judo will be available three days a week but not on Friday when there will be aerobics instead and there will be yoga on three days but on Monday there will be a karate class. For the time being, the centre will not be open on Saturday and Sunday although it is hoped...

HEALTH AND FITNESS CENTRE TIMETABLE

	Monday	Tuesday	Wednesday	Thursday	Friday
6.30 - 9.00	weight-training table tennis snooker	weight-training table tennis snooker	weight-training table tennis snooker	weight-training table tennis snooker	weight-training table tennis snooker
	open to all	open to all	open to all	open to all	1
12.00 - 2.00	2	4	6	8	weight-training aerobics yoga
	3	5	7	9	staff only
5.00 - 9.00	10	12	14	16	18
	11	13	15	17	19

PLEASE NOTE: The Centre is . . . . 20 at weekends

(20 marks)

2 APPROACH

In this question, you have to complete a table, flow chart, organization chart, timetable, questionnaire or form of some kind. Numbers are not necessarily involved, although they may be a secondary aspect of some questions. The table (or other document) will be less complex in design than in Question 3 and the emphasis is on completing it rather than understanding it. This means that there will be a second element in this question, which contains the information needed to complete the table. In most cases this will mean that you have to compare a passage (containing information) with an incomplete table. Your task is to transfer the information accurately from one place to another. The table, or document, will display the information in a clearer and more concise manner than the prose passage. Essentially, this question involves re-ordering of given information.

Provided you are careful and pay attention to detail, Question 4 should be fairly straightforward.

You will sometimes be instructed to copy the table into your answer book. For this reason, it is useful to bring a ruler. At other times, there will be numbers in the table and you must write the number and your answer next to it in your answer book. Do not complete the table on the question paper, except as part of your rough work.

If a part of the table is already completed, study it carefully to see how you should continue.

When you complete the table, you will be writing down single words, short phrases, dates and numbers but not usually complete sentences.

Do not be put off by the sometimes unusual appearance of this question. It is easier than it seems and requires no creative thought. A careful and methodical approach can gain you high marks.

As with all questions, read through your answer carefully to be sure that it makes sense. Check also for accuracy in using words which appear on the uncompleted table or elsewhere in the question, as misspelling of words given to you will be penalized.

3 MODEL ANSWER

1   *female staff only*
2   *weight-training, aerobics, karate*
3   *staff only*
4   *weight-training, table tennis, snooker*
5   *staff only*
6   *weight-training, aerobics, yoga*
7   *female staff only*
8   *weight-training, aerobics, yoga*
9   *staff only*
10   *weight-training, judo, karate*
11   *open to all*
12   *weight-training, table tennis, snooker*
13   *open to all*
14   *weight-training, judo, yoga*
15   *staff only*
16   *weight-training, judo, yoga*
17   *female staff only*
18   *weight-training, aerobics, yoga*
19   *open to all*
20   *closed*

4 COMMENTS ON MODEL ANSWER

This answer is wholly correct and would receive full marks.

- The writer has followed precisely the instruction about how to present the answer.
- She has looked at the completed sessions to see what is required and has used this information to help her with the uncompleted parts of the timetable. She has also looked carefully at the specimen answers and has copied the form while realising that they are not correct.
- Probably this writer began by writing *weight-training* in every slot, since it is clearly stated that this activity is always available.
- The next step would be to fill in the *staff only* and slots for lunchtime sessions, since this information is fairly clear.
- The examination paper could be used to work things out in rough.
- By tackling the straightforward parts of the table first, a considerable number of marks has already been obtained.
- By the time the writer gets to the more difficult parts at the end of the minutes, most of the spaces have already been filled in.
- The writer has tackled the timetable as a whole and not attempted to complete each answer fully before starting the next one.

5 SECOND ANSWER

1 open to all   2 weight-training, yoga, karate
3 weight-trianing, aerobics, karate

All lunchtime sessions are for staff only with Wednesdays reserved
for female staff.

6 COMMENTS ON SECOND ANSWER

This is rather a disastrous attempt at the question which could not be given more than 2 marks.

- The writer has again written his answers across the page instead of down it.
- He has mistakenly copied the specimen answers, even though they are incorrect.
- He has copied undigested extracts from the question.
- He has spelt words from the passage inconsistently, both correctly and incorrectly.
- What has happened here is that the writer has not understood the nature of the task and has given up. Probably he tried to answer the numbered questions by looking for the information in the passage. Such a technique would work for Question 2, but for this question it is better to start with the passage and transfer the information to the timetable piece by piece, gradually building it up. In this way, many of the answers would be partly completed at any given time. This is a better approach than trying to find the complete answer to one question before proceeding to the next.

7 SUMMARY OF COMMON ERRORS

APPROACH

- Not understanding the task to be performed.
- Taking an ineffective approach; for example, trying to fill specific gaps in a table rather than beginning with the information provided by the passage and spreading it throughout the table as appropriate.

PRESENTATION

- Not presenting the answers as requested, i.e. not using the number system given, or failing to copy out a table if requested.
- Writing answers confusingly across the page.

LANGUAGE

- Misspelling of key words given in the passage or the incomplete table.

8 FURTHER PRACTICE

Situation: Mr Thomas Brown, who lives in Manchester, is going on a two-week skiing holiday in Europe. His wife Mary, his daughters Rachel, aged 14, and Sarah, aged 16, who are all very keen skiers will be going with him. He has asked you to complete his application for travel insurance, for him to sign today.

Task:　Complete the form according to the information given. Make up any further information that you need.

Application Form

Surname and initials of insured persons	Premium per person
1	
2	
3	
4	
5	
6	
Total premium	

Areas: (See premium rates) Please tick (✓) box for cover required
1 ☐ 2 ☐ 3 ☐　　Winter sports required ☐

Date of departure _____ Date of return _____

Address of first named person _____

_____

1. A cheque/postal order for the total premium is enclosed ☐
2. I authorize you to debit my account ☐

Account number ☐☐☐☐☐☐☐☐

Branch _____

_____　　Sort Code - -

Signature _____　　Date _____

Premium rates per person

*Areas	Up to 5 days		6 - 10 days		11 - 18 days		19 - 31 days		Each additional week or part up to 3 months	
	Adult	Child	Adult	Child	Adult	Child	Adult	Child	Adult	Child
1. UK and Isle of Man	£6.50	£4.85	£6.50	£4.85	£8.00	£6.00	£10.50	£7.85	Available on request	
2. Channel Islands, Rep of Ireland, Europe, Mediterranean Islands, Morocco, Algeria, Tunisia, Libya, Egypt, Israel, Lebanon, Jordan, Syria, Turkey, Madeira and Canary Isles.	£8.00	£6.00	£10.50	£7.85	£11.50	£8.60	£16.00	£12.00	£3.65	£2.75
3. Worldwide	£24.00	£18.00	£24.00	£18.00	£24.00	£18.00	£28.00	£21.00	£6.50	£4.85

*Rates for children apply to those under 16 at date of departure, accompanied by an adult insured on the same certificate. The above rates exclude winter sports but this cover can be included at three times the above rates.

MARKING SCHEME AND ANSWERS

1	Brown, T	£34.50	2
2	Brown, M	£34.50	2
3	Brown, S	£34.50	2
4	Brown, R	£25.80	2
	Total Premium	£129.30	1
	Areas	tick in box 2	1
	Winter sports	tick in box	1
	Date of departure	appropriate date	1
	Date of return	a date two weeks after first date	1
	Address: Mr Thomas Brown		1
	address including number and street		1
	Manchester		1
	EITHER a tick in box for cheque OR tick in debit		
	account plus account number and branch address		2
	No signature		1
	Today's date		1
	Total		**20**

FURTHER PRACTICE QUESTIONS

In some English for Business First Level papers all four questions relate to one common theme, such as office re-organization, company policy, or travel arrangements. The four questions still have their own individual characteristics, however, and a paper with a common theme is not fundamentally different from a paper in which each question has a different topic.

The four questions that follow are about business opportunities in East Yorkshire, which is in the North-East of England in an area where the local authority wishes to attract new companies.

A marking scheme for each of the questions, and correct answers to questions 2, 3, and 4, are given at the end. The questions may be attempted and checked against the marking scheme one by one, as in the earlier sections of the book, or else written as a practice paper for examination purposes.

QUESTION 1

Situation: You work for an international company which has many European subsidiaries, including one in the South of England. At present you are working in the English subsidiary.

The Managing Director of the English company has seen some advertisements in the press about opportunities for companies to move or expand their operations into East Yorkshire, in the North-East of England. He has asked you to write a letter, for him to sign, asking for more information.

Task: Write the letter. Address it to Mr Neil Bravey, Industrial and Economic Development Officer, The Town Hall, Bridlington, East Yorkshire YO16 4LP. In your letter, you should say something about your own company, say why you are writing, ask for more information about locating in East Yorkshire, request any brochures or video films that may be available, enquire about any financial assistance the local authority may be able to offer, and suggest the possibility of a visit to the area in the near future.

Lay out the letter correctly and make up any necessary information.

(30 marks)

QUESTION 2

Situation: The employees of your company have been informed and consulted about the possibility of moving to East Yorkshire. You have been asked to speak at a meeting at which they will ask you questions about life in East Yorkshire. You do not have to answer questions about working conditions (your colleague Mr Slater will deal with that area) but only about the social aspects of life in East Yorkshire, such as housing, education and amenities.

Task: Read the information leaflet and write down the answers that you gave to the questions that people asked at the meeting.

Note: Your answers to the following questions should be brief but give all the information required.

1   What opportunities are there for watching professional sport in East Yorkshire?

2   I have heard that classes in schools are very large. Is this true?

3   What sort of housing is available for young people who have just got married?

4   Are there any buildings of historical interest in East Yorkshire?

5   How many people live in East Yorkshire?

6   Are you sure that the beaches in East Yorkshire are clean?

7   What new developments are there in Bridlington?

8   What kind of house could I buy for £100,000?

9   Does Bridlington have first-rate shopping facilities?

10   Is East Yorkshire a good place to bring up children?

11   I have heard that as a holiday resort Bridlington is declining and fewer and fewer tourists are going there. Is this true?

12   Will there be any changes in salaries and working conditions when we move to East Yorkshire?

(30 marks)

East Yorkshire is one of the most pleasing areas in the north of England. It has a population of approximately 81,400 and covers 104,367 hectares. It is a district of great character and outstanding natural beauty and has rich, rolling farmland, unspoilt villages, busy market towns and clean, sandy beaches. The administrative centre is at Bridlington, (population 30,960) which is a popular holiday resort, port and residential town. Bridlington's newest attraction is the multi-million pound Leisure World Complex. This was one of the reasons why Bridlington was chosen by the English Tourist Board as the resort most likely to succeed in the 21st century. East Yorkshire also has a superb 12-mile stretch of fine clean beaches which made Bridlington the winner of the 'U.K. Top Award for Cleanliness'. There are many places of historical and scenic interest, such as the beautiful old country houses of Sledmere and Sewerby Hall, the fine gardens of Burnby Hall and the lighthouse and high cliffs at Flamborough.

Not only is East Yorkshire one of the most desirable places in which to live but its house prices have in recent years been considerably lower than the national average. A detached four-bedroomed house can be purchased for around £75,000 and very fine houses in a rural setting with extensive land are no more than £100,000. At the lower end of the market, semi-detached and terraced houses on modern estates start at around £45,000. It is also possible to buy land on which you can build your own house, or have one built to your own design, and there are many old houses which can be purchased cheaply and renovated. We are also very proud of our academic institutions. The teacher/pupil ratio is amongst the best in the country and our children's academic achievements are very good.

East Yorkshire has many new roads and there are superb leisure facilities, including horse-racing, ice-skating, first-class football and the new marina in Bridlington Bay. There is a new shopping centre in Bridlington itself and extensive shopping facilities in the large cities of Hull and York, which are within easy reach.

QUESTION 3

Situation: You have been asked to provide a summary of the population
structure and distribution in East Yorkshire, using statistical
information.

Task: Using the information in the table, fill in the spaces in the paragraph
below. Your answer may be a word or a number.

Note: A parish is a number of villages grouped for administrative
purposes.   (20 marks)

There are (1) . . . . females than males in the population of East Yorkshire.
(2) . . . . of the population are under the age of fifteen and nearly the
(3) . . . . number have retired. Housewives make up approximately 16
(4) . . . . cent of the population. The number of full-time workers is not
known but if we include part-time workers then the working population numbers.
(5). . . . . If we look at the latest figures, it appears that since 1971 the
total population has (6) . . . . by (7) . . . . to 81,400.

There are four towns in East Yorkshire, the smallest of which is (8) . . . .

Approximately (9) . . . . people live in these towns. The

(10). . . . . of the population live in villages, which are grouped into
parishes. In the list the (11) . . . . parish is Stamford Bridge and Fangfoss
has the (12) . . . . population. Not (13) . . . . the parishes
are listed here - there are another (14). . . . . , all of

(15) . . . . with (16) . . . . inhabitants than the ones on the
list. The larger parishes include villages where there are schools and

(17) . . . . which attract people from the (18) . . . . villages.

These figures may not be totally reliable because some are (19) . . . . and
(20) . . . . are out of date.

Current Population
Provisional figures (1987) indicate that the population of the Borough of East Yorkshire is 81,400.

Towns:

Bridlington	30,960
Driffield	9,600
Market Weighton	4,030
Pocklington	6,040

Larger Parishes:

Bempton	930
Flamborough	1,960
Skipsea	600
Beeford	810
Hutton Cranswick	1,840
Kilham	890
Middleton-on-the-Wolds	820
Nafferton	1,820
North Frodingham	730
Wetwang	650
Barmby Moor	950
Bishop Wilton	470
Fangfoss	360
Melbourne	550
Stamford Bridge	2,780
Sutton-upon-Derwent	410
Wilberfoss	1,540

(The above list of parishes contains the larger villages which, because they contain a primary school and some shops, tend to act as minor centres for the remaining parishes within the Borough of which there are 47)

Population Structure
(Because the latest figures have not been analysed in terms of age and sex structure, these figures are from the 1971 census)

Children under 15, male and female	13,700
The work force (including part-time workers)	28,000
Retired people	13,000
Housewives and others	10,800
Total	65,500
Males	31,200
Females	34,300

QUESTION 4

Situation: You have been asked to prepare a table which gives information about a number of sites in East Yorkshire. Your company may move to one of these sites.

Task: Study the information in the following advertisements and summarize it under the appropriate headings in the table. The table has been partly completed and you should complete the numbered spaces. If the information is not in the advertisements, write 'not stated'.

Name of site	Nearest town or village	Nearest road	Site available	Essential Services	Housing nearby
Hutton Cranswick	Hutton Cranswick	A164	5 acres	Yes	not stated
Kellythorpe	1	2	3	4	5
Skerne Road	6	7	8	9	10
Pocklington	11	12	13	14	15
Full Sutton	16	17	18	19	20

(20 marks)

Commercial and Industrial sites in East Yorkshire

Kellythorpe Industrial Estate
This new industrial estate lies close to the Driffield by-pass which forms part of the A163. Although near to the by-pass the site is within two miles of Driffield town centre. There is planning permission for 32 acres to be developed for industrial use.

Skerne Road Industrial Estate
This estate is conveniently sited within the built-up area of Driffield, which has good shopping facilities, and a wide range of both older and modern houses. The site covers 20 acres of which 5$\frac{1}{2}$ acres has planning permission and is available for development now. Essential services are available.

Hutton Cranswick Industrial Estate
This estate is 4 miles south of Driffield and very close to the expanding village of Hutton Cranswick from which it is separated by the Driffield to Beverley road (A164). The estate comprises 21 acres of which 5 are available for immediate development. Essential services are available.

Pocklington Industrial Estate
The estate is close to the Hull-York road (A1079) and very near to Pocklington, an attractive market town which in recent years has diversified economically and has experienced considerable residential growth which has led to a thriving housing market. The extent of the estate is some 72 acres and there are 8 acres of land immediately available for development. All essential services are available.

Full Sutton Industrial Estate
This estate covers part of a former airfield. Three miles to the west is Stamford Bridge, a large pleasant village on the River Derwent with a fine range of housing, shops and a school. Two miles further west lies York and four miles to the south-east is Pocklington. The site is approximately 40 acres in extent and largely developed and occupied, but there are a number of small sites available.

MARKING SCHEME FOR QUESTION 1

Content (fullness, accuracy, relevance, creativity etc.)

Brief description of company	3
Give reason for writing	3
Request for information	3
Ask about financial assistance	3
Possibility of a visit	3

Language

Mechanical accuracy (deduct half mark for error but do not penalize for the same error twice).	7
Appropriate style for a business letter	3

Layout

Mr Bravey's name and address	1
Name and address of the writer's company	1
Dear Mr Bravey	1
Date	1
Yours sincerely + name + position (ignore presence or absence of signature)	1

30

MARKING SCHEME AND ANSWERS FOR QUESTION 2
2 marks for answers 1 to 6. 3 marks for answers 7 to 12.

Answers that are partly correct may be given less than the maximum for each answer.

1 It is possible to watch horse-racing and first-class football.
2 No, not at all. East Yorkshire schools have one of the best teacher/pupil ratios in the country.
3 House prices start at around £45,000 for modern semi-detached and terraced houses.
4 Yes, there are the beautiful old country houses of Sledmere and Sewerby Hall.
5 The population is 81,400.
6 Yes, because Bridlington was the winner of the 'U.K. Top Award for Cleanliness' because of its clean beaches.
7 There is a new multi-million pound leisure centre, a new shopping centre and a new marina in Bridlington Bay.
8 You could buy a very fine house in the country with plenty of land.
9 It has a new shopping centre, but it is quite a small town. However, it is easy to get to the large cities of Hull and York.
10 Yes, because it has good schools, fine beaches and attractive countryside.
11 No, Bridlington has been chosen by the English Tourist Board as the resort most likely to succeed in the 21st century, which means that tourism is likely to increase.
12 My colleague Mr Slater will answer that question.

MARKING SCHEME AND ANSWERS FOR QUESTION 3
1 mark for each correct answer.

1 more
2 13,700
3 same
4 per
5 28,000
6 increased
7 15,500 (allow any number within 500 either side)
8 Market Weighton
9 50,600 (allow any number between 50,000 and 60,000)
10 rest, remainder
11 largest, biggest
12 lowest, smallest
13 all
14 47
15 them
16 fewer
17 shops
18 smaller
19 provisional
20 others

MARKING SCHEME AND ANSWERS FOR QUESTION 4
1 mark for each correct answer.

1	Driffield	11	Pocklington
2	A163	12	A1079
3	32 acres	13	8 acres
4	not stated	14	available
5	not stated	15	Yes
6	Driffield	16	Stamford Bridge
7	not stated	17	not stated
8	5½ acres	18	small sites available
9	available	19	not stated
10	Yes	20	Yes

London Chamber of Commerce and Industry Examinations

How to make contact

Address   London Chamber of Commerce and Industry Examinations Board
Marlowe House
Station Road
Sidcup
Kent
DA15 7BJ
England

Telephone (from within UK) 081 302 0261
(from outside UK) + 44 81 302 0261

Telex   888941 LCCIG ATTN EXAMS BOARD

Facsimile (from within UK) 081 302 4169
(from outside UK) + 44 81 302 4169

If you need	*Contact ....*
1 Information or advice on the English for Business or English for Commerce examinations of the LCCI, or on examining centres	Dr G D Pickett Examinations Officer Languages and EFL
2 Past papers of the examinations	Publications Department
3 Details of the Spoken English for Industry and Commerce (SEFIC) oral examination	Dr G D Pickett
4 General information on the LCCI Commercial Education Scheme and Examination Board, or on examinations other than English for Business or English for Commerce	Publications Department
5 More detailed information on specific, non-English examinations	The relevant Examinations Officer